FINANCIAL INDEPENDENCE

1.

'A big part of financial freedom is having your heart and mind free from worry about the what-ifs of life.'

Suze Orman

Financial independence actually has much less to do with the amount of money which you have than the attitude you have towards it. In other words, as long as you have enough to enjoy life and not worry about any emergencies, it could be argued that you are financially free. However, working on the principle that a little more would be welcome, it is necessary to see how we can increase our wealth. And that's what the rest of this book will do.

Financial Independence. David Hirst

2.

'Pleasure in the job puts perfection in the work.'

Aristotle

erfection in the workplace usually gets noticed. And to get going on the road to financial independence you will need to be noticed to get the opportunities to increase your income. With the increased income you can then invest and generate further income. But it all has to start somewhere, and that place is taking pleasure in what you do so you do it well.

Financial Independence. David Hirst

3.

'*Choose a job you love, and you will never have to work a day in your life.*'

Confucius

Financial independence is arguably having enough money to do what you want when you want and how you want. If you really love what you do, it is a pleasure, a joy, and one that you don't consider work. So, if you can find an activity that you love and one which can generate an attractive income, you are one of the successful people who can actually say they have achieved the beginnings of financial independence.

Financial Independence. David Hirst

4.

'Your chances of success are directly proportional to the degree of pleasure you desire from what you do. If you are in a job you hate, face the fact squarely and get out.'

Michael Korda

One of the most successful ways of achieving financial independence is to set up your own business. However, the key criterion here is that you must love the industry you move into: there must be passion and enjoyment. If you are setting up in an industry you know to be profitable, and that is your only reason for doing so, then you will not be as successful as a person who truly enjoys the work. In fact, there is a good chance of failure if money is the only reason for entry to the business. Love what you do or, as the quote suggests, get out and find something else.

Financial Independence. David Hirst

5.

'*When I was young, I thought that money
was the most important thing in life; now
that I am old I know that it is.*'

Oscar Wilde

It is never too early to start investing a portion of your income. To start your journey towards financial freedom you will need some sort of investment vehicle, and that will require initial capital. Essentially there are three ways forward: invest some of the salary you currently get; move to a position/company that can generate an income large enough for you to invest part of it; borrow from a bank/venture capitalist/family/other etc. to invest. The latter is the least advisable. Then you can look at the plethora of investment possibilities including setting up your own business.

Financial Independence. David Hirst

6.

'You never get every job you want.'

Mackenzie Astin

O nce you realise the truth of this, it is much
easier to start looking for promoted
positions either in your current company or
others. I have found that generally people like to stay
secure in their comfort zones and only apply for
posts that they can easily do. While there is some
merit for this, you should also consider posts that you
don't know everything about as they will often
provide training and support for you to do a good
job. Also, some jobs that initially don't seem so
interesting may actually turn out to be quite
motivating when you know more about them.
Besides, if the real goal is financial independence
then you will need to know as much as you can about
the boring aspects of a profession as well as the
interesting parts too.

7.

'We must start with the reality that corporations cannot guarantee anyone a lifetime job any more than corporations have a guarantee of immortality.'

John W. Snow

Another fantastic quote that helps us realise that we should always be looking to improve ourselves to be more valuable to the company should there be another recession or retrenchments. We should also see that no job is permanent and no person indispensable, so even if you really love what you do, we should still keep an eye open for other opportunities in other companies. This will also help give you a measure of your worth in the marketplace which is very valuable information when it comes to salary negotiations.

Financial Independence. David Hirst

8.

*'The price of success is hard work,
dedication to the job at hand, and the
determination that whether we win or lose,
we have applied the best of ourselves to the
task at hand.'*

Vince Lombardi

The road to financial independence is not
paved with gold; it is paved with hard work.
Anyone who tells you that they became
financially independent with ease is either lying or
they love what they're doing so much that it didn't
seem like hard work at all. Find out what your
strengths are, and they are usually the things you like
doing, and apply them to your work. Once you have
achieved financial independence, you might look
back on it and say it wasn't that difficult, but actually
you will need to work hard to get it. The reward is
worth it.

Financial Independence. David Hirst

9.

'When you are asked if you can do a job, tell 'em, 'Certainly I can!' Then get busy and find out how to do it.'

Theodore Roosevelt

When you find yourself in the position of an interview either for a new job or a promoted post, always project a positive and self-confident image. If you hesitate or cast doubt on your ability, the interviewers will remember that doubt in the final evaluation. However, there is a distinction between lying and being positive. Lying, is knowing you can't but saying you can. Self-confidence is thinking you might be able to and wanting to try. Enthusiasm will win the day.

Financial Independence. David Hirst

10.

'I was very afraid that I wouldn't be able to do this job well. And the time never came back.'

Sharon Olds

Once you commit yourself to becoming financially independent, and this becomes your main focus in whatever you do, you will quickly discover that you can achieve an amazing amount of progress in a fairly short space of time. Fear will try and hold you back, but this is just coming face to face with the unknown. Once you try something for the first time it becomes less fearful; and when you've tried it several times it can become a skill.

Financial Independence. David Hirst

11.

'A lot of people quit looking for work as soon as they find a job.'

Zig Ziglar

I'm amazed how many people give up on life so easily. As soon as they manage to land a half-decent job with a reasonable income, they seem to give up the idea of bettering themselves and/or looking for other opportunities. I believe that as soon as you get a half-decent job, this is exactly the time to focus on what the *next* stepping stone is to financial independence. Never give up searching for better opportunities, but do remember to smell the roses along the way.

Financial Independence. David Hirst

12.

'We can create the ultimate job security by becoming less dependent on the organization for which we work and more dependent on our own resources.'

Bo Bennett

The more reliant you are on something, the more dependent you are too. It's like investments: if you have all your savings in one investment vehicle, you are very dependent on it doing well. However, if you have a varied portfolio, you create more options for yourself and are less vulnerable to potential threats. The same applies to the workplace. If you know your worth in the marketplace and you keep observant to openings in other companies, you create potential options. Therefore, in the event of a disaster and retrenchments, you will know where to apply, who to apply to, and what type of positions to apply for. Just because it's not advertised doesn't mean that it doesn't exist for the right person. Good companies are always on the lookout for talent.

Financial Independence. David Hirst

13.

'No man ever listened himself out of a job.'

Calvin Coolidge

Listening is the most important skill to ensure you do well. So many employees make the fundamental mistake of trying to impress the boss by telling them all the things that they've done, all their accomplishments, and their abilities. The person who really impresses management the most is the one that can listen well and encourage the boss to talk.

Financial Independence. David Hirst

14.

'It is easier to do a job right than to explain why you didn't.'

Martina Navratilova

A move in the right direction to financial freedom is to put effort into everything you do. This could be at work or in your social life, but the point is that putting effort into things to ensure you doing them right every time is an excellent habit to get into. This is the habit that financially independent people learn first: putting in effort to get things done right. Those that don't put in the effort end up doing a half-hearted job that often needs correcting later. And then you have to explain to management why it wasn't done right in the first place, which is always a step backwards.

Financial Independence. David Hirst

15.

'Work harder on yourself than you do on your job.'

Jim Rohn

Without a doubt, the best investment you will ever make is in yourself. Invest in your education, your health, your fun, and your relationships. Investing in *you* will always, without fail, give the best returns. So, irrespective of whatever job you have, constantly look for ways to improve yourself.

Financial Independence. David Hirst

16.

'What I tell these young people is, the world is not as dangerous as the older generation would like you to believe. Anyone I know who has ever taken a risk and lost a job has ended up getting a better one two years later.'

Jonathan Kozol

This is one of the key quotes to achieving financial independence: risk is not only unavoidable; it should be encouraged in measured doses. Anything you have ever achieved in your life that is of any value to you has necessitated taking risk. For example, a degree, a car licence, a marriage. They have all required you to take risk – some more than others. But without risk, there will be very little learning and very little hope of achieving financial independence. Of course, nobody likes failing, but as the quote suggests: the learning curve you get from not being successful far outweighs the loss.

Financial Independence. David Hirst

17.

*'If you want to make an easy job seem
mighty hard, just keep putting off doing it.'*

Olin Miller

You will often hear people who have set up their own business mention that they wish they had done it sooner. Or that they wish they had left their previous company sooner. Of course it's easy to look with hindsight, and difficult to predict the future, but I would urge everyone to avoid putting off the tasks that they know will take them closer to financial independence. And that often means taking the very difficult decision to step outside your comfort zone and make a plan to move to another company or start your own business.

Financial Independence. David Hirst

18.

'A lot of it, as it is in any job in life, is being in the right place at the right time.'

Julie Harris

This is so true, so always keep looking for opportunities as they won't always come looking for you. It may also be possible to create opportunities too by making carefully considered suggestions. I remember one fresh graduate on the company's trainee management development programme presenting a proposal to management who, in turn, liked the project so much they created a new team of people to complete it. They also promoted the fresh grad as team leader of people twice his age and experience. It is an example that you can change your situation by *you* creating the right place at the right time.

19.

'The best way to lose a job is just not to care. When you do not care, it shows in everything you do.'

Bo Bennett

Not every business which is set up is successful the first time round. And sometimes, to replenish the savings or capital, you need to return to the job market and work for someone else. This is why it's always a good idea to care about everything you do and keep on very good terms with your previous employer. You never know if you might need a reference from them in the future. And if your business is successful, they might also become your customer.

Financial Independence. David Hirst

20.

'You don't concentrate on risks. You concentrate on results. No risk is too great to prevent the necessary job from getting done.'

Chuck Yeager

If you want to make a better life for you and your family, you will need to take measured risks. And the bigger reward you want, then the greater the risks are likely to be. My advice is to take a few smaller risks first to get a feel of the pressure and how you cope with the stress. Then, look at the results you want to achieve and measure the risks associated with them. Then evaluate your appetite for risk and take the appropriate path. A personal recommendation is the middle path of reasonable risk for reasonable reward.

Financial Independence. David Hirst

21.

*'It's the job that's never started takes longest
to finish.'*

J. R. R. Tolkien

If you see your life's ambition as achieving financial independence, then the sooner you start planning for this, the sooner you will achieve the result. Several of the quotes in this book are related to procrastination, and the reason for this is that it is the single most inhibiting factor to achieving your goals in life. It all becomes so much easier once you start, but making the start is the area that most people fail.

Financial Independence. David Hirst

22.

**'Oh, you hate your job? Why didn't you say
so? There's a support group for that. It's
called everybody, and they meet at the bar.'**

Drew Carey

This quote reminds us to stop complaining and get on with life. In particular, it's saying that if you don't like your job, do something about it. For some that might mean going to a bar and sharing your dreams of how life could be with others. However, the real success stories are those who get on and make a plan to live their dreams. And it often starts with the smallest of achievements.

Financial Independence. David Hirst

23.

'You'll be old and you never lived, and you kind of feel silly to lie down and die and to never have lived, to have been a job chaser and never have lived.'

Gertrude Stein

One of the most, if not *the* most shameful phrases is 'I wish I had...' It gives the impression that you had the intention to do something but just never got around to doing it. It's shameful because, you know that you could have done something, but you chose not to. People who say this type of phrase will always try and blame it on something outside of their control, but the truth is that it was always within their influence, but they just never bothered. If your goal really is financial freedom, then you need to *do* something about it now. Otherwise it will be too late sooner than you think.

Financial Independence. David Hirst

24.

'Amidst all the clutter, beyond all the obstacles, aside from all the static, are the goals set. Put your head down, do the best job possible, let the flak pass, and work towards those goals.'

Donald Rumsfeld

nce you have established your goals and made them 'SMART' – specific measurable, acceptable, realistic and time-bound – you can then get on with achieving them. For sure there will be obstacles that get in your way, and unfortunately some of these will actually come from people you know. They will be jealous of your success because your success will reinforce the failure in *their* lives. Ignore their negativity and distractions as best you can and focus on *your* goals.

Financial Independence. David Hirst

25.

'A real job is a job you hate.'

Bill Watterson

So often people do the same job for years and years, yet they hate it. And the more they do it the more they hate it. The justification and excuse for this irrational behaviour is financial dependency. These people use words like 'have to' and 'got no choice'. They have resigned themselves to being dependent on others and will therefore never achieve true financial freedom. If you are in this position, the first thing to do is recognise that you do have options, and the first should be to look online for something else.

Financial Independence. David Hirst

26.

'The biggest mistake that you can make is to believe that you are working for somebody else. Job security is gone. The driving force of a career must come from the individual. Remember: Jobs are owned by the company; you own your career!'

Earl Nightingale

You own your career. You have choice. You can make a difference to your life and the life of those around you. Most of the very successful people today started out with less than you. Yet they have made it to become financially independent, famous (if that's what you wish), and have the life that many dream of. What's the difference between these people and you? I think the difference is this: they started living their dreams by committing themselves to doing something about their situation.

Financial Independence. David Hirst

27.

'I learned to take the first job that you have in the business that you want to get into. It doesn't matter what that job is, you get your foot in the door.'

Wes Craven

To really be successful in something may necessitate an element of sacrifice. I know a florist who gave up a very well-paid job in HR to work part-time in a florist's as an assistant to learn the trade. It required quite a lot of sacrifice to live on a much lower wage and eat into her savings. However, she became not only so much happier than before, she has now set up her own on-line business and is on her way to achieving the success that will ultimately pay better than the job she left. She got her foot in the door, learnt as much as she could and then took a risk to start her own business.

Financial Independence. David Hirst

28.

'I have more than a job: I have a purpose.'

David Hirst

The people who are most successful in their job are the ones that enjoy what they do. To gain financial independence from the company you currently work in, you must discover something you love about what you do. Without this passion your bosses and company decision makers will sense that there is something insincere about you and pass you over for another when it comes to moving up in the company.

Financial Independence. David Hirst

29.

'Happiness is not in the mere possession of money; it lies in the joy of achievement, in the thrill of creative effort.'

Franklin D. Roosevelt

Having money on its own is not intrinsically important; it's what money can do that is useful. Financial independence lies not in a specific amount of money, but in a feeling of comfort. A feeling that if you see something you'd really like, you have the means to go out and get it. That could be a Maserati, or just a pair of shoes. The chances are that the new pair of shoes will come first. However, if you truly desire a fast car, then you can have that as your main goal. I suspect though, that once you have enough money to afford it, you will choose not to buy it. Sometimes having the dream and working towards it, is even nicer than the reality of achieving it.

30.

Money often costs too much.

Ralph Waldo Emerson

It has never been easier to become financially independent than now. Access to information is far greater than it has ever been, and with information comes knowledge and ideas. However, if the desire for money is so great that it obscures the other far more important elements of your life such as family and friends, then the cost is too great. Obtaining money will always require hard work, determination and sacrifice, however, if the sacrifice becomes too great then the money costs too much.

Financial Independence. David Hirst

31.

'The safe way to double your money is to fold it over once and put it in your pocket.'

Frank Hubbard

There are a lot of so called 'get rich quick' schemes out there. And the majority are designed to make the person who invented it even richer. Pyramid schemes such as Multi-level marketing are a typical example. If you get in at the beginning, you rely on other people to create your (passive) income for you. However, the chances of this are very slim. It is far more likely that you will be the one creating the passive income for someone else higher up the chain. Be very wary of anyone who tells you that you can make a fortune easily because it takes effort, more effort, and just a little bit of luck.

Financial Independence. David Hirst

32.

'Focusing your life solely on making a buck shows a poverty of ambition. It asks too little of yourself. And it will leave you unfulfilled.'

Barack Obama

Financial independence is an excellent goal, but there has to be a game plan for when you achieve it. Money is not useful in itself: there has to be something more attached to the value of having it. After all, it's only useful if you can do something with it. Satisfying ambition is the driving force to success which will ultimately be far more rewarding than counting the amount of money you have. If your ambition is to have an exclusive property without any loan, it will feel so much more rewarding when you achieve it than wanting a million dollars and achieving a figure.

Financial Independence. David Hirst

33.

*'Can anybody remember when the times
were not hard and money not scarce?'*

Ralph Waldo Emerson

Money will always be scarce, but I often hear that it was easier in the past. To a certain extent I can understand their point of view, because they are looking at the past from the knowledge perspective they have in the present. So, many things in hindsight look obvious; however, they probably weren't at the time of them taking place. People in the future will surely say that it was easier to make money today than in the future. The reality of it is to focus on the positive achievements so far and the bright future to come, and avoid negative or pessimistic thought.

Financial Independence. David Hirst

34.

'There is a very easy way to return from a casino with a small fortune: go there with a large one.'

Jack Yelton

R econcile the fact that there is no easy way to
financial independence for the majority of
us. The lottery ticket winners are few and far
between; they exist, of course, and continue to buy
one if you feel lucky, but the best way to spend your
time is planning and acting out those plans.

Financial Independence. David Hirst

35.

'My problem lies in reconciling my gross habits with my net income.'

Errol Flynn

This is a great play on the word 'gross', but there is a very good message here if you are serious about achieving financial independence. Get rid of some of your bad habits – and most people have them. Cigarettes and alcohol can be expensive habits; and so can mistresses, toy-boys and compulsive shopping. Do you really need to buy that cake, that packet of cigarettes, that bottle of gin? For a start, add up the amount of money you spend in a year on tobacco, alcohol or online splurge shopping and see what it amounts to. Then set yourself a target to invest a portion of that amount for the next year.

Financial Independence. David Hirst

36.

*'I am opposed to millionaires, but it would
be dangerous to offer me the position.'*

Mark Twain

undamentally I see two types of people: those who will achieve financial independence and those who will not. They are easy to recognise as they make it obvious for all to see. If there is a very expensive car such as a Ferrari, Rolls Royce, or such, the person who wishes to scratch or damage it out of spitefulness or jealousy will never achieve financial freedom. However, the person who looks at the car, admires it, and decides that one day he or she will have one too, will.

Financial Independence. David Hirst

37.

'There's no money in poetry, but then there's no poetry in money, either.'

Robert Graves

oney for its own sake is redundant: it has no intrinsic beauty (except, perhaps, to numismatists). First decide what your definition of financial freedom is, because it will be an individual interpretation. Then check to see if it's specific and realistic. After this, create a working plan to achieve it. The plan is almost sure to change as you go along because you will want or need different things in your life. But the important part is that you have started the journey, however old you are.

Financial Independence. David Hirst

38.

*'After a visit to the beach, it's hard to believe
that we live in a material world.'*

Pam Shaw

When you consider your definition of financial freedom, bear in mind that most, if not all, of the most beautiful things in this world are available with little money. The cost involved is far more likely to be the emotional involvement. An absolutely magical time can be had at a candlelit dinner. Likewise, sitting and watching the changing light on the edge of a Norwegian fjord can be a breath-taking event. Or even relaxing on a beautiful beach. Sometimes we need to take stock of what's really important to us, and then incorporate these into our future plans. Remember to stop occasionally to smell the flowers.

Financial Independence. David Hirst

39.

'Life is a game, and no-one gets out alive.'

Neil Campbell

This quote comes from a person who I greatly admire as someone who understands the machinations of life. Neil sees that financial independence is as much, if not more, an academic exercise as it is to do with gathering money. There is a stark reality to it in terms of having an income (passive or otherwise) that allows you the freedom to enjoy the heart's desires. But there is also an incredibly powerful factor to it: no-one gets out alive. The message is to really appreciate what you have and, when you plan what you'd really like, then think carefully about the time it will take to achieve it. We all have a sell-by date.

Financial Independence. David Hirst

40.

*'When I have money, I get rid of it quickly,
lest it find a way into my heart.'*

John Wesley

ollowing on from the previous quote, if you would like one of those super yachts that the billionaires have in Monte Carlo, but would be very happy with a schooner, consider the schooner first. Once you own it, your goals will change. You might like to save enough to take a sabbatical and live for a year on a (rented) yacht. Your savings would certainly become depleted, unless you picked up part-time work on the way. But what an experience you would have, and this would last a lifetime. You would, without doubt see things differently on your return. And, even with the depleted savings, you would most certainly be closer to achieving financial independence.

Financial Independence. David Hirst

41.

'There are people who have money and people who are rich.'

Coco Chanel

The irony is that you can have a lot of money but not really be rich, or really appreciate what to do with the money. The answer is to invest in learning. The more you learn, the more you are able to appreciate the finer things in life. A vintage bottle of Bordeaux can taste the same as a cheap house wine to a person who cannot appreciate the difference. So, perhaps ignorance is bliss? No, for the discovery of new things can be an excellent journey to a greater happiness.

Financial Independence. David Hirst

42.

'Waste your money and you're only out of money, but waste your time and you've lost a part of your life.'

Michael Leboeuf

art of financial independence is having the freedom to do the things you want to do. And these things will change as time passes by. When people are young, they exist without really considering time and what they do with that time. So much of it is wasted when it could be used to work towards a debt free future. Reading is a good start for anyone, but particularly the young. For the not so young, time has an even higher value, so spend it wisely: make sure that something makes you smile and laugh everyday – have fun.

Financial Independence. David Hirst

43.

'*A bank is a place that will lend you money
if you can prove that you don't need it.*'

Bob Hope

It seems that many people think of banks as safe,
benevolent and kindly institutions designed to
help you towards financial independence.
However, they are businesses and as such they wish
to extract as much a profit as they can for themselves
and their shareholders. To do so they must get your
money and make it work for them. The true path to
financial freedom is not through a bank's
investments, it's through your own. Banks can give
you a helping hand if you're lucky, but they will
exact a heavy price in the form of interest.

Financial Independence. David Hirst

44.

'I'm so poor I can't even pay attention.'

Ron Kittle

There are some people who give up on financial independence because they have so many debts, obligations and no time for anything else but the present. My advice is this: go without something, perhaps (if there is nothing else) even lunch for a couple of days, then treat your family (just your partner if not enough), then do it again, but this time spend it on yourself. A book, perhaps, or an online training course or something that will increase your knowledge about your work. Then, do the same again, but this time look into your future and decide.

Financial Independence. David Hirst

45.

'A tragic irony of life is that we so often achieve success or financial independence after the chief reason for which we sought it has passed away.'

Ellen Glasgow

It is unfortunate that many people only achieve financial independence later in life. And in this case, they no longer want to have the low-slung sports car, nor the powder snowboarding adventure escape in the alps, or even hiking in the Amazon jungle for a few months to help discover new species. As we age our goals change: it is also quite common that the closer we get to our dreams, the dreams change – this is quite natural. Nevertheless, the important part is to generate goals that are so powerful that they motivate you to do something about achieving them. So, the chief reason why we started may pass, but allowing them to change will help you attain them.

Financial Independence. David Hirst

46.

'People may take a job for more money, but they often leave it for more recognition.'

Bob Nelson

L ike most things in life, financial independence has a price, and for some that price is a bit too high to pay. For example, it will take hard work and probably not happen overnight, so this is why some people feel that they earn enough money for a reasonably good life and other things start to take a higher priority such as family, friends and perhaps recognition for what they do or who they are. But, then again, you could also argue that these people have already found a type of financial independence as money is low on their priority list.

Financial Independence. David Hirst

47.

'The economy depends about as much on economists as the weather does on weather forecasters.'

Jean-Paul Kauffmann

Once you have an amount to invest in your future, you will face a barrage of people who wish to help you do so. Many of these investment advisers will promise you magnificent returns for your capital, and these will be very attractive. But be wary, you have to ask yourself if the true role of these people is to make money for you or to make money for themselves and/or the organization they work for. Usually it's the latter. Listen to the views of economists, but don't trust them completely. Invest in something *you* believe in because there is a very high chance that others will believe in it too, and therefore it will be a success.

Financial Independence. David Hirst

48.

***'October: This is one of the peculiarly
dangerous months to speculate in
stocks. The others are July, January,
September, April, November, May, March,
June, December, August and February.'***

*Mark Twain, Pudd'nhead Wilson's Calendar
for 1894*

This quote is a wonderful summary of the advice you can get from investment advisers. These so-called experts will promote a number of investment vehicles as if they are the most wonderful things since sliced bread. But always, they will add a disclaimer at the end. In other words, they are making educated guesses about what they think the markets will do. In one case I was advised by a bank to invest in X, and then a well-respected investment house adamantly stated exactly the opposite. The answer is to educate yourself by listening to as many people as possible, and trust your own summary.

Financial Independence. David Hirst

49.

'If money is your hope for independence, you will never have it. The only real security that a man will have in this world is a reserve of knowledge, experience, and ability.'

Henry Ford

Money in itself will never guarantee independence; that, in essence, is a frame of mind. Further, as you gather wealth, you will want more and more. So, when do you achieve true financial independence? It's when you have the knowledge and wisdom to appreciate that you have arrived at a stage of happiness and the means to maintain that happiness.

Financial Independence. David Hirst

50.

'A dollar picked up in the road is more satisfaction to us than the 99 which we had to work for; and the money won at Faro or in the stock market snuggles into our hearts in the same way.'

Mark Twain

Another wonderful quote by Mark Twain that shows how the human condition so likes something for nothing. At the end of the day, financial freedom comes from hard work and then investing the profits of that hard work into something that will generate further and sustained wealth in the future. Some people may be luckier than others and if you feel you're in this category then by all means go out and buy a lottery ticket.

Financial Independence. David Hirst

51.

*'It is natural that affluence should be
followed by influence.'*

*Augustus William Hare and Julius Charles
Hare. 1827*

It is also possible to add that it is natural that knowledge should be followed by affluence. There are many ways to become affluent, but the easiest is to develop your own knowledge. Get a book, read and devour the contents as if the information it contains will one day save your life. Listen to a podcast that adds to your comprehension of a subject. Watch a television programme that increases your understanding of something. Above all, enjoy the learning experience as this is one of the keys to financial independence.

Financial Independence. David Hirst

52.

'A woman's mink coat represents the sacrifice of a lot of little animals, including her husband.'

Mignon McLaughlin

Unless you are lucky enough to inherit a fortune, to get anything of any significance you will have to make sacrifices. The most valuable of these will be your time, not money, so spend it wisely. This is why it is important to start the learning/education process as early as possible. The earlier the better, but it's never too late because it's also important to remember that the learning experience should never stop. If it does, then so will your life.

Financial Independence. David Hirst

53.

*'It is better to have a permanent income
than to be fascinating.'*

Oscar Wilde

There are those that crave attention and stardom, and those who like to be the centre of attention and admired. They make themselves as fascinating to others as possible, and love to be the topic of conversations. However, this is really a lonely existence, and as Oscar Wilde suggests, it is far better to forget the fame and go for the fortune.

Financial Independence. David Hirst

54.

*'If all the economists were laid end to end,
they'd never reach a conclusion.'*

George Bernard Shaw

I once listened to an economist talk for about an hour about the future for investors, but actually say very, very little of substance. A friend had the courage to ask what everyone else was thinking: What should we invest in and when? We were then treated to another half an hour of everything but the answer. So, we left the seminar grateful for the free dinner, but none the wiser for what we should invest in other than ourselves at the bar. Actually it is worth listen to these talks, but always keep focussed on your goal of getting clear answers to specific questions.

Financial Independence. David Hirst

55.

*'Empty pockets never held anyone back.
Only empty heads and empty hearts can do
that.'*

Norman Vincent Peale

If you have an idea and the enthusiasm to follow it through, there will always be some people to help you achieve your goal because they will have an interest to make sure you are successful. The two items holding you back are an empty head – a lack of education, information and knowledge; and an empty heart – the passion, the fuel to get on and do something about your ideas and dreams. Having a lack of money at the start is a poor excuse not to start.

Financial Independence. David Hirst

56.

'Rule No.1: Never lose money. Rule No.2: Never forget rule No.1.'

Warren Buffett

All investments have risks attached to them –
even very safe ones such as fixed bank
deposits. However, once you factor in
inflation you may find that you are, at best, just
maintaining your investment. If inflation is higher
than your percentage return, then you are losing.
Some investments offer the possibility of very high
returns, but the downside is the higher risk. But there
is an answer: if you never want to lose money, invest
in yourself.

Financial Independence. David Hirst

57.

'Diversify your investments.'

John Templeton

There are some who swear by property as an investment. However, I know several people who have lost a substantial amount of money on property either as an investment or as a place to live. Some people say invest in unit trusts, and I know people who have lost almost 40% of their investments with them. Other people say invest on the stock market, and we all know people who have lost. But if you're in the right place at the right time you can make a killing. So, to be a little more on the safe-side invest in a variety of investment vehicles.

Financial Independence. David Hirst

58.

'The time of maximum pessimism is the best time to buy and the time of maximum optimism is the best time to sell.'

John Templeton

Another great quote because most people invest the other way around. They hear how their friends are doing, because people always like to talk about how much they are making, and they would also like a piece of the action. I know of one person who invested in a stock that had done very well for one of their friends and lost a considerable amount when it fell the following week. Very few investors like to admit they have lost, and everyone likes to be thought of as a winner. However, when the market is down and people have lost a lot, then this is probably the best time to enter the market.

Financial Independence. David Hirst

59.

'Only buy something that you'd be perfectly happy to hold if the market shut down for ten years.'

Warren Buffett

Unless you are a speculator that follows every movement of the market, I would advise potential investors to follow the above advice. Stocks will go up and down, but generally, over the long term, they will go up if you can hold. A particularly good piece of advice is to invest just after the market has bottomed out after a fall, then hold until you can see a good gain from your investment.

Financial Independence. David Hirst

60.

'Literature is an investment of genius which pays dividends to all subsequent times.'

John Burroughs

This quote again supports the notion that the best investment you can make is in your own learning. And when you do get advice from 'experts' you will be in a better position to ask the type of knowledgeable questions that will give you the answers you need to invest as wisely as possible.

Financial Independence. David Hirst

61.

'Investors have very short memories.'

Roman Abramovich

We all live in hope for a better future, and we can often be heard saying that our childhood was the happiest time of our lives. Then again, in reality it probably wasn't, it's just that we are conditioned to just remember the good times. And this is the same with investing. We all like to forget the bad times and therefore create hope. Remember the stock market will fluctuate and it will go down – probably after it has gone up for some time.

Financial Independence. David Hirst

62.

'He's a serial entrepreneur. Somebody stop him before he makes a killing again.'

Carl Zetie

This is a great reminder that the majority of people who achieve financial independence at an early age are those who have started their own businesses. Even if you feel unsure about starting something on your own while you have family and other obligations, consider setting up a part-time business and see how it goes. In any event, the learning curve will be high from a minimal investment, and you will probably have fun trying your hand at a business you enjoy.

Financial Independence. David Hirst

63.

'We go to school to learn to work hard for money. I write books and create products that teach people how to have money work hard for them.'

Robert Kiyosaki

chools used to condition us right from an early age to think about getting a job, getting married, having '2.2' kids, buying a house and retiring gracefully on a pension. Things have changed and we are encouraged to set up our own businesses more. Society is also more tolerant of differences so that a couple can be acceptable even if they don't want children, or want to get married. We are also now encouraged to look at wealth differently and develop a passive income where the money works hard to generate more money. It's a far easier way to financial independence.

Financial Independence. David Hirst

64.

'Live as if you were to die tomorrow; learn as if you were to live forever.'

Mahatma Gandhi

There is always the question of how long should I budget for? How long do I expect to live? And this leads to the perennial dilemma of should you treat yourself to that something nice now or should you save the money for your retirement? It's an impossible question to answer because everyone's circumstances will be different. Nevertheless, the above quote is a wonderful ideal, although practicality suggests that it's also a good idea to create some savings that can help you generate further income.

Financial Independence. David Hirst

65.

'The question is not do you take money out of stocks and put it into real estate, or the reverse. There's so much money out there looking for a home. I don't think it's either/or.'

Sam Zell

The key to making your hard-earned money work for you is to invest wisely. The question is: What does 'wisely' mean? You can ask twenty people and get twenty different answers, but unless you have a particular field of excellence to tell if an industry will do better than others, I'd recommend diversifying your portfolio. Not too wide; make sure that there is a reasonable sum invested in each one so that you will be able to see a tangible result. And then study so you are better informed for future investments.

Financial Independence. David Hirst

66.

*'There are no rules about investment.
Sharks can be good. Artist's dung can be
good. Oil on canvas can be good.'*

Charles Saatchi

When considering what to invest in, as well as more conventional investment vehicles, think out of the box and also consider collectables. Sometimes the return on these types of investments can far out-strip their traditional counterparts. Especially consider this option if you are also a collector of sorts as you will have a better knowledge of what is likely to appreciate than many others. Wine, art of all sorts, fish etc. In fact, all collectables have an investment value. And it can be so much more fun too.

Financial Independence. David Hirst

67.

'As in all successful ventures, the foundation of a good retirement is planning.'

Earl Nightingale

Start planning now with a specific long-term goal. Then fix some specific dates that you intend to achieve certain realistic medium-term goals that will lead you towards the long-term goal. Finally, set some short-term goals and give them specific dates for completion and make them achievable. The first of these short-term goals should be the completion of these plans, share them with your family and friends and also share what penalty you will pay if you don't achieve them. This should help with your commitment.

Financial Independence. David Hirst

68.

'The question isn't at what age I want to retire, it's at what income.'

George Foreman

The very idea of retirement gives the impression that you suddenly stop whatever you're doing, and that's wrong. If you stop doing things you'll die of boredom. One of the concepts of financial freedom is that you earn money doing what you would do anyway if you had the free time. It's also true to say that financial freedom is a different figure to different people. If you are happy with your current lifestyle, and are not in debt, and can maintain that lifestyle without working for someone else, then you can truly say you are financially independent.

Financial Independence. David Hirst

69.

'Age is strictly a case of mind over matter. If you don't mind, it doesn't matter.'

Mark Twain

ge is a relative thing. I have met teenagers who look and act as if they were in their mid-forties. I have also met some seventy-year-olds who acted like teenagers. If you don't mind that some narrow-minded people may criticise you, then it doesn't matter. Bear in mind that even if you behave age appropriate, there will still be people who will criticise you. So as long as you're happy and you avoid hurting anyone else's feelings, then why not behave as you wish? Enjoy life.

Financial Independence. David Hirst

70.

'All my possessions for a moment of time.'

Elizabeth I

Time is the most precious commodity.
Therefore, if you are not using it to become
financially independent, then you should be
enjoying every moment of it. The best scenario is, of
course, a combination of the two.

Financial Independence. David Hirst

71.

'I want a house that has got over all its troubles; I don't want to spend the rest of my life bringing up a young and inexperienced house.'

Jerome K. Jerome

any families wish to own a new property and feel that this is the best way to make the most of their investment money. But in many countries, you have to spend a considerable amount on renovating the place before you can call it a home. It will also have some teething problems, if you're lucky these will be minimal. Consider a pre-owned property that has all these problems over with. And if you wish to purchase a place to rent out, first consider a place you would like to live in and then target like-minded people. If you find it hard to rent out at a price you're happy with, then you still have a place that you are happy to live in.

72.

'The only way of discovering the limits of the possible is to venture a little ways past them into the impossible.'

Arthur C. Clarke

The idea of financial independence is seen by many as a dream that is unlikely to happen: they have trouble seeing beyond their current situation. And this is a shame as freedom is possible, even probable, if you set your mind to it. The task is to bring the dream – the so-called impossible – to reality by focussing on how you can improve yourself and your situation, and this is often achieved by reading and investing in a learning experience. Venture into the impossible by learning how to do the things you've never done before.

Financial Independence. David Hirst

73.

'It's better to live rich than to die rich.'

Henry David Thoreau

There are those who are prepared to do something they hate for a short period of time to get closer to financial freedom. And this is fine providing you ensure that it is a temporary sacrifice you're making. The risk is that you convince yourself that you need more and more so you stay doing something you hate doing for longer. Whatever you do, ensure you enjoy life because you never get a second chance at it.

Financial Independence. David Hirst

74.

'Nothing is free. Always trade.'

David Hirst

I t's true for negotiation and it's true for life and your time. Whenever you do something for someone, make sure that you get something in return. That could just be a smile, a fun time, or a favour at a later date; it could be money or assistance with something you need. The important point is to always negotiate with your surroundings and the opportunities that come into your life for a better future.

Financial Independence. David Hirst

75.

'If you want to be a writer — stop talking about it and sit down and write!'

Jackie Collins

Likewise, if you want to be financially independent stop dreaming about it and get on with identifying your goals and making plans to achieve them. Don't wait! Put this book down and do it now.

Financial Independence. David Hirst

www.ingramcontent.com/pod-product-compliance
Lightning Source LLC
Chambersburg PA
CBHW070903160726
48004CB00003B/1222